YOUR KNOWLEDGE HAS

The Evolution of the Female Detective in Crime Fiction. A Journey of Feminism

GRIN ☺

Bibliographic information published by the German National Library:

The German National Library lists this publication in the National Bibliography; detailed bibliographic data are available on the Internet at http://dnb.dnb.de.

ISBN: 9783346779717
This book is also available as an ebook.

Print and binding: Books on Demand GmbH, Norderstedt, Germany
Printed on acid-free paper from responsible sources.

The present work has been carefully prepared. Nevertheless, authors and publishers do not incur liability for the correctness of information, notes, links and advice as well as any printing errors.

GRIN web shop: https://www.grin.com/document/1307355

University of Constance
2016
Faculty of Literature
American Crime Fiction

The Female Triumph in Crime Fiction
a Journey of Feminism

Table of Contents:

1. Introduction   1

2. Defining Terminology   3

3. The Evolution of the Female Detective – a Journey of Feminism

     3.1 Amelia Butterworth: The First Female Detective   3

     3.2 Kinsey Millhone: The Breakthrough   7

     3.3 Kay Scarpetta: The Modern Female Detective   15

4. Conclusion   21

5. Bibliography   23

1. Introduction

Every generation has had their fair share of representative spokespeople who have stood up for the feminist movement. Alice Stone Blackwell, Betty Friedan and Yoko Ono only constitute the tip of the iceberg. Superficially, the feminist movement has come a long way since the 18th century. Especially on a political level, women have gained more and more rights. Women are now allowed to own property, they are allowed sole custody of their children and since 1920, women are permitted to vote in political elections. However, full equality is still a work in progress and by no means fully achieved yet.

Simply googling the words "feminism today" will give you 36.000.000 results. This substantial number suggests that the issue is everything but outdated or irrelevant. Today's role models of the feminist movement are especially young female celebrities, including Amber Rose, Lena Dunham, Ellen Page and Emma Watson and politicians such as Michelle Obama and Hillary Clinton.

The prevailing relevance of the issue can be discerned from the following excerpt from Emma Watson's speech during an event for the HeForShe campaign in 2014. In her speech Watson references a different speech held by Hillary Clinton:

"In 1995, Hilary Clinton made a famous speech in Beijing about women's rights. Sadly, many of the things she wanted to change are still a reality today" (UN Women, 2014).

These two women, who are of different ages, have different backgrounds and very different careers speak out about the same issue, more than 50 years apart from each other.

A phenomenon as important as the feminist movement will of course also find its way into literature. It is a well acknowledged fact that literature functions as a mirror of society. Literature changes and evolves just as much as the society within which it has been created. The setting and content of a novel written by a Nigerian peasant in 1865 will probably differ strongly from those written by a British aristocrat in 1950. In consequence, the female protagonists of a novel from the 18th century will differ in many aspects from those that appear in a novel written from today's point of view.

The following term paper will use novels of the genre crime fiction to illustrate the evolution of female protagonists – in this specific case – female detectives. This genre is especially interesting because it was associated very male characteristics for most parts of its existence. The development of this genre, which lead us to today's variety in gender amongst detectives, is an accurate representation for the evolution of the feminist movement. In other words, female crime writers had to enter a domain dominated by men just as much as their female protagonists had to enter a profession that was formerly exclusively occupied by their male counterparts.

We will start by briefly defining the terms used throughout this term paper. The main part will be structured chronologically, with the beginnings of the female detectives during the 18th century up until today's representatives of the genre. In order to prove that the image of the female detective has changed simultaneously with the development of the feminist movement, we will take a closer look at three distinct crime fiction novels. The literature we chose will focus on female detectives in novels written by women authors from the United States. Moreover, these female detectives are to some extend archetypes of their respective fields. Lastly, we will conclude our findings by giving a concise summary and analyzing whether full equality among female and male detectives in crime fiction has been established.

2. Defining Terminology

"Defining feminism presents a challenge as great as defining crime fiction" (Reddy, 1988, p.9), but for reasons of clarity and comprehension these two terms shall be briefly explained.

In the following paper, the term 'crime fiction' will be used as a generic term including all fiction that involves solving a murder, including hardboiled crime fiction, the noir genre, locked room mysteries and whodunits.

Furthermore, the term 'female detectives' will be used as an umbrella term for any female protagonists that are involved in solving crime, be it professionally or otherwise. This includes private investigators, police consultants and forensic scientists.

The term feminism and the women's rights movement are described as the emancipation of American women, containing any battle to enhance their status socially, politically, economically, and in respect to their self-concept. In comparison, the women's rights movement is more tightly defined as the winning of legal rights as part of the emancipation of women (see Lerner, 1971, p. 236).

3. The Evolution of the Female Detective – a Journey of Feminism

3.1 Amelia Butterworth: The First Female Detective

When thinking about the term crime fiction, most people will automatically associate the names Sherlock Holmes or C. Auguste Dupin, and Arthur Conan Doyle or Edgar Allan Poe with it respectively. Clearly, those are male characters created by male authors. However, the first detective narratives were written earlier than one might assume. In fact, the earliest stories of the genre were written by women for other women, the so called "domestic detective fiction". Those very first crime stories were created long before Arthur Conan Doyle started to bring back the excitement for the detective story in the late 1800s and early 1900s. "A native tradition of the genre flourished in the work of women writers who used the detective story to explore and defend domestic ideology"(Cassuto/ Eby/Reiss, 2011, p. 804).

Without question, the first fictional detectives of significance were Dupin and Holmes, but this paper will focus on the rise of female detectives written by female writers and how feminism influenced this phenomenon. Furthermore, the first female detectives were created by male authors as well, but for the purpose of this paper we will disregard those also.

The appearance of the first fictional female detective, Amelia Butterworth, dates back to 1897. She was created by Anna Katharine Green and made her debut in the novel *The Affair Next Door*. Amelia Butterworth can be categorized as a female amateur detective, a type of detective that can mostly be found in narratives before 1945.

Green can not only be considered the forerunner for female novelists to write detective fiction in general, but more importantly to introduce the female protagonist, the female detective to the genre. Therefore, she has been attributed the title "Mother of Detective Fiction" (Maida/Green, 1986, p. 53).

Amelia Butterworth can be regarded as the prototype for earlier and today's female detectives. She is described as a curious and observant single woman who spends her time with following her interest in solving murders. Butterworth is the perfect example of the so-called spinster sleuth, "a woman who is unmarried, especially a woman who is past the usual marrying age [...] with time on her hands and an observing eye" (Herbert, 1999, p. 423). Butterworth's first steps into solving crime happen accidentally. When she notices suspicious activity in her neighbour's house, she informs the police and refuses to give up until they agree to investigate the case.

From the beginning, Miss Butterworth is presented as the type of woman who challenges the traditional female characteristics. First of all, she has never been married and lives by herself.

Secondly, when confronted with a dead body for the first time, she keeps her countenance, while a stereotypical woman probably would not stay as calm, as the following quote illustrates:

> "At a sight so dreadful, and, in spite of all my apprehensions, so unexpected, I felt a sensation of sickness which in another moment might have ended in my fainting also, if I had not realized that it would never do me to lose wits in the presence of a man who had none too many of his own" (Green, 1897, p. 26).

Later in the novel it becomes clear that Miss Butterworth's help in solving the crime is not wanted and she has no right to interfere with police investigation, but she does not relent and finally works alongside the responsible police detective Mr. Gryce.

Amelia Butterworth has various motives for detecting crime. Firstly, she feels obliged to protect her neighbourhood and secondly, it is a welcome distraction from the monotony of her life.

She is driven by her believe in justice and desire to protect the innocent, especially young women mistreated by their husbands and suitors (see Ross, 2010, p. 34).

Additionally, Green emphasizes the rivalry between men and women by pitting Amelia Butterworth against the police detective Ebenezer Gryce. Throughout the whole story she has to stand up against Gryce's condescendence, but she is not intimidated by his contempt. An example for the prejudices Butterworth is confronted with is the scene where she figures out that the victim's hat has only been worn once and she mentions that "[t]here was a murmur about me, whether of amusement or displeasure, I made no effort to decide" (Green, 1897, p.72). She has to constantly struggle with being taken seriously by men, because the way she solves crimes seems to adhere to female intuition and instinct rather than classical intelligence and deductive skills.

Not only is she not intimidated by her male opponent but is rather convinced that she is the better detective and therefore does not hold back when it comes to voicing her opinion.

At some point she proclaims that "[she has] noted something today which [she thinks] has escaped [Mr. Gryce]" (Green, 1897, p.128), implying that she is the more attentive and consequently the better detective of the two. The rivalry between Gryce and Butterworth thematises the battle of the sexes. Bringing up this specific topic in literature has raised more awareness for the problems women often have to face, which can already be seen as a great step for feminism.

Green has always addressed social issues in her novels. One theme she consistently occupies herself with is the exposure of injustice, mostly towards women (see Maida/Green, 1986, p. 56). From today's perspective, the connection of the progress of female detectives and the emancipation of women, in this case American women, is very prominent.

Furthermore, her intention was to show that women are not subordinate to men and can sometimes even be superior in most, if not all aspects. Moreover, she challenges tradition by letting women work in the same field as men. During the time the story is set, 1895, it was impossible for a woman to be part of the police force, let alone to be an active part of a murder investigation. Through breaking those traditions in her works, Green challenges the fixed image society had of women at that time. Women started to see that they could be more than just housewives or spinsters, and thus were inspired by the strong female character.

Literature was one of the triggers that caused women to start to take a stand for their rights, and slowly break out of their traditional roles, in order to achieve more freedom and self-determination. With time, the number of women who joined this movement increased.

Moreover, in the 1960s the first consciousness-raising and self-help groups for women emerged in the United States. Women started to take matters into their own hands instead of waiting for men to do so for them. Those were the first steps for feminism and the women's rights movement to build up momentum and to gain more importance, not only in literature but also in real life.

The resulting changes in the perception of women were precipitated and mirrored by events such as

> "the establishment of a Presidential Commission on the Status of Women in 1961; the publication in 1963 of Betty Friedan's immensely influential Feminine Mystique, with its indictment of systemic sexism in American society; the passage of the American

Equal Pay Act of 1963 and the Civil Rights Act of 1964, which prohibited sex discrimination in employment and mandated a government agency to enforce its policies; and the incorporation of the National Organization for Women (NOW) in 1966" (Walton/ Jones, 1999, p. 12).

The above-mentioned events were part of an era known as the second wave of feminism.

Even though the first American female detective might have already been born as early as 1897, the breakthrough of successful female detectives did not take place until the 1980s.

Between 1914 and 1945 the American hard-boiled detective dominated the American crime fiction genre. In his manifest for hard-boiled writing *The Simple Art of Murder* Chandler even explicitly states "that the predominant figure in any novel which dared to depict American society at its worst could only be male" (Bradford, 2015, P.90).

Therefore, female detectives like Sarah Keate by Mignon G. Eberhart, Millicent Newberry by Jeanette Lee and Gale Gallagher by Will Ousler and Margaret Scott did not experience the success they might have deserved.

3.2 Kinsey Millhone: The Breakthrough

The turning point for the recognition and success for female detectives arrived during the 1980s. So far the female detective had undergone a great transformation from its beginning in 1897. The female detective genre, also referred to as private eye genre, which has developed in the 1980s has been powered by "a nostalgia for the idealistic social action of the 1960s and early 1970s, when the women's movement (and activism more generally) seemed to hold so much promise for changing both society as a whole and individual lives" (Walton/ Jones, 1999, p. 34).

The most noticeable changes of the female detective are her character and her demeanour. The heroines are illustrated as more well-rounded, complex and realistic characters. Additionally, the new generation of female detectives are more engaged in political and social issues, which has as a result that the themes addressed in the novels are more reflective of the issues and problems American society was facing at that time (see DellaCava, 1993, p. 3). The protagonists of crime fiction were now confronted with topics that were of actual relevance for US citizens such as drug abuse, gay rights or A.I.D.S. With time, the female detective reflected society even more realistically, which in turn made it easier for American women to identify with her.

Although the topics of feminism, emancipation and the women's rights movement had already been important for writers before, it was only during the 1980s that those topics became a crucial issue. The best examples for this era of female detectives are Sharon McCone, Kinsey Millhone and V.I. Warshawski by Marcia Muller, Sue Grafton and Sara Paretsky, respectively. They can be seen as "pioneering constructions of the modern female detective figure" (Ross, 2010, p. 148). Authors such as Sara Paretsky, Marcia Muller and Sue Grafton have strategically rewritten the patriarchal history of the American hard-boiled detective novel of the 1930s and 40s (see Walton, Jones, 1999, p. 4). Furthermore, these authors started to feature strong central women characters with which women of the time and ever since could easily identify.

By now relocating women into the world of crime and mystery solving, these authors break with old stereotypes and free women from their traditional roles. Instead, they give their heroines strength, power and moral authority. As Sarah Paretsky said, she and all other women writers have the goal "to broaden the range of their voices, to represent their age for women, to describe women's social position – and their triumphs" (Ross, 2010, p. 40).

Another interesting point is that since the 1980s the number of female detectives has significantly risen. This may be connected to the increase of female authors choosing to create a female detective as their novel's protagonist (see DellaCava/Engel, 1993, p.80). Marcia Muller's Sharon McCone is one of them. She works for the legal firm All Souls Legal Coop, and is thus the first female investigator who makes her living as a detective, as supposed to merely doing it as a hobby like Amelia Butterworth did. Her character's profession marks a new milestone of feminism, namely the possibility for women to enter a field which used to be reserved for men, such as that of an investigator at a law firm. The woman's domain has changed from the private sphere to the public sphere. Women were not chained to the stove anymore; housekeeping was no longer their *raison d'être*. The growth in number of fictional female detectives reflects a simultaneous growth of the rising acceptance of employed women in American society (see DellaCava/Engel, 1993, p.15).

Additionally, other current topics of the 1980s such as divorces, young widowhood, death of a child, and family crisis were often brought up and processed in literature. With women taking on professions formerly reserved for men, sexism at the workplace became another major issue. The female detectives Kinsey Millhone and V.I. Warshawski by Sue Grafton and Sara Paretsky represent the next step in the development of female detectives as well as feminism, since both characters are strong and independent women who are self-employed detectives with their own agency.

The following portion of this paper will illustrate the development of the female detective by focusing on Kinsey Millhone as an example for the simultaneous evolution of both, feminism and crime fiction.

Kinsey Millhone first appears in 1982 in the crime novel *A is for Alibi* by Sue Grafton. She is one of the first female detectives to be self-employed. Therefore, she functions as an example of a woman that is independent and self-sufficient in her professional life.

Kinsey Millhone is introduced with the opening paragraph "[my] name is Kinsey Millhone. I'm a private investigator, licensed by the state of California. I'm thirty-two years old, twice divorced, no kids" (Grafton, 1993, p.7). From the very beginning Grafton makes sure that her readers know who they are dealing with. This introduction helps the reader to identify more easily with Kinsey Millhone; she is an ordinary woman just like her female readers are. Furthermore, she is relatable because some of her readers may share experiences with her such as the process of going through a divorce.

Sue Grafton states that Kinsey Millhone is licensed at the very beginning of the novel, which means she is a professional investigator and has the right to do detective work. This shows a

9

considerable development from the first amateur detective Amelia Butterworth who did not officially have the authority to solve cases. Later in the story the reader learns that Millhone used to be a police officer but did not enjoy the job. She wanted to be more independent and not, as she explains, have to "[work] with a leash around [her] neck" (Grafton, 1993, p. 19). Moreover, she did not want to have to justify herself and constantly ward off the sexist insults from her male colleagues. Even though women might have already been allowed to work in the police force and also in other mostly male dominated positions, they had to withstand "a variety of problems best summarized as sexism in employment" (DellaCava/Engel, 1993, p.32). Just because women were now permitted to work in those areas, did not mean they were welcomed there.

Sue Grafton continues with introducing Kinsey Millhone as follows:

> "The day before yesterday I killed someone and the fact weighs heavily on my mind. I'm a nice person and I have a lot of friends. My apartment is small but I like living in a cramped space. [...] I live in one room, a 'bachelorette'. I don't have pets. I don't have houseplants. [...] Aside of the hazard of my profession my life has been ordinary, uneventful and good. Killing someone feels odd to me and I haven't quite sorted it through" (Grafton, 1993, p. 7).

Although Sue Grafton was evidently inspired by the characteristics of a hard-boiled detective, she adds further details and depth, which goes to show that her protagonist is more than just a simple imitation of the male tradition (see Ross, 2010, p.148).

Characteristics of the hard-boiled detective which Kinsey Millhone displays are for example that she does not seem to have any family relations, she lives in a minimally furnished apartment, drinks alcohol regularly and carries a gun. Furthermore, the story takes place in an urban setting similar to that of hard-boiled fiction. In addition, Sue Grafton pays homage to one of the most prominent authors of hard-boiled detective fiction Dashiell Hammett by naming a dog after him (see Grafton, 1993, p. 38).

In opposition to the hard-boiled tradition, she maintains a social life outside of her profession which includes meeting friends and having to deal with everyday chores such as grocery shopping, housecleaning, doing laundry and even shaving her legs. These mundane activities make Kinsey Millhone an ordinary American woman. This in turn is one of the reasons why her character is so appealing to the female readers of the 1980s; they can easily identify with her. Moreover, she struggles with personal issues, for example her beginning relationship with Charlie Scorsoni, and her feelings of guilt for the death of Sharon Napier. In a nutshell, Kinsey Millhone is a human being with common problems and feelings just like every other American woman.

The introduction of a relatable detective is a new feature of crime writing, where the investigation is no longer the sole focus of the plot. Instead, the reader needs a hero to identify with who explains more than just the case, but also the social and political situation of the time (see Bertens/ D'haen, 2001, p. 59). Sue Grafton does exactly that. She shifts the focus from the investigation to the investigator. She uses her hero Kinsey Millhone to show women that they can break out of the traditional image of females and be independent as well as strong. Kinsey Millhone is characterized as a woman with a mind of her own; she even admits that she can be a "bitch sometimes" (Grafton, 1993, p. 207) and that she "never has been good at taking shit, especially from men" (Grafton, 1993, p. 205).

Moreover, she represents the exact opposite of the stereotypical woman. Firstly, she is not married but twice divorced; she has no children and lives in a small apartment on her own. Secondly, housework does not seem to be very important to her; she cannot cook and only does the laundry and goes grocery shopping when it is necessary. Lastly, she does not care about being fashionable; in her opinion, jeans, t-shirt and a blazer are a perfectly fine outfit.

Furthermore, Sue Grafton also deals with fairly representative issues of the 1980s such as divorce, the loss of children and parents as well as sexism in employment, which were also important issues for the feminist movement.

The subject of divorce is already mentioned in the first paragraph of the novel and runs through the whole story like a golden thread. Not only Kinsey Millhone but also other important characters like Nikki Fife and Gwen are divorced.

> *"[When] the marriage blew up, I was totally unequipped to deal with the real world. He managed the money. He pulled the strings. He made the major decisions, especially where the kids were concerned. I bathed and dressed and fed them and he shaped their lives. I didn't realize it at the time because I was just running around to please him. [...] I sound like all the other women who came out of marriages in that era."* (Grafton, 1993, p. 41),

Gwen says to Kinsey when they meet for the first time. She continues by telling how she fought for the custody of her children but eventually lost. With this scene Grafton wants to stress that women should not solely depend on a man and that it is crucial for women to keep their independence during marriage. This excerpt seems to be an appeal for women to have the courage to stand up for themselves and not be scared of voicing their opinion. This notion is emphasized when Kinsey Millhone says: "That's when you give the other guy half of what is rightfully yours. I've done that lots of times. It sucks" (Grafton, 1993, p. 207). It is indicated that women should not always have to compromise. The reader is warned not to make Millhone's mistakes and rely too heavily on a male partner, especially in relationships where male and female are not equal.

Another central topic is the sexism Kinsey Millhone has to experience. She started her career at the police academy, but as mentioned above she did not like to "work on a leash" (see Grafton, 1993, p. 19) and to deal with the daily sexist comments. But even as an independent, self-employed detective she has to cope with the prejudice against females as detectives and women in general. During one incident she asks Lieutenant Dolan from the Homicide Department for information, and he replies: "You'd get more out of me if you'd learned to flirt" (Grafton, 1993, p. 17). Kinsey's answer to that is "[no] I wouldn't. You think women are a pain in the ass. If I flirted, you'd pat me on the head and make me go away" (Grafton, 1993, p. 17). This excerpt shows a woman's dilemma. If women used their sexuality for their advantage, they would not be taken seriously. However, if they tried to work professionally, they would not succeed either. It seems that as a woman, you cannot get it right. Both ways to deal with the situation would be met with sexist responses. Kinsey Millhone represents all women who are discriminated against by their male and even female colleagues because of their gender.

In her novels, Sue Grafton also deals with the physical disadvantages women supposedly have in a sarcastic manner. Kinsey Millhone indicates during a surveillance that "[one] of [her] old cohorts used to claim that men are the only suitable candidates for surveillance work because they can sit in a parked car and pee discreetly into a tennis-ball can, thus avoiding unnecessary absence" (Grafton, 1993, p. 35). Ironically, she leaves her surveillance work afterwards because she has to use the bathroom but makes clear that "[the] basic characteristics of any good investigator are a plodding nature and infinite patience. Society has inadvertently been grooming women to this end for years" (Grafton, 1993, p. 36). It is indicated that society has made women the better investigator by accident. Grafton illustrates through Kinsey Millhone that not all attributes that men claim to be of disadvantage necessarily have to be that. Some female characteristics can in fact be beneficial for the detective work. In this specific case: A woman's patience.

Another characteristic that is often ascribed to females exclusively is empathy. Grafton demonstrates to her female readers that it is perfectly fine to have and to show emotions and that is does not automatically constitute weakness. When Kinsey Millhone visits Libby's mother Grace she starts to cry at one point. Millhone who has no children can still feel for her and her eyes start to water as well. Here, a different topic of the time has been picked up, namely the loss of a child. Another example for her empathy is how Millhone feels about Sharon Napier's death. She feels guilty because she did not arrive at the place where they were supposed to meet in time and is thinks that she maybe could have avoided the murder if she were.

Moreover, Sue Grafton encourages women to trust their instinct and gut feeling. Although, Kinsey Millhone is trained in her profession, she still trusts her instincts, as did Amelia Butterworth, and they mostly turn out to be right.

At the end of the novel, she trusts her instincts and confronts Grace with the accusation that she killed Laurence and Grace confesses to the murder. Furthermore, her gut feeling tells her that there is more to the story, and she does not ignore that hunch. Eventually, when "it just popped into [her] brain and it fitted" (Grafton, 1993, p. 236) she figures out that Charlie Scorsoni has been involved in the crime as well.

The Kinsey Millhone series by Sue Grafton was a great success. With every book of the series she developed her character more thoroughly and encouraged women to be like Kinsey Millhone, independent and strong. Some indication for her success might be found on the New York Times best-seller lists. In 1990 her seventh novel *"G" Is for Gumshoe* stayed on the hardcover best-seller list for seven weeks. Her earlier novel *"F" Is for Fugitive, in* turn, stayed on the paperback best-seller list for eight weeks. All of her subsequent novels made it onto both best-seller lists (see Walton, Jones, 1999, p. 11).

The transformation from the first American detective Amelia Butterworth to Sue Grafton's Kinsey Millhone has been immense and so has the evolution of feminism thus far. With Amelia Butterworth not only the first American female detective was created but also the highly significant subject of feminism found a medium to reach women in America and to awake a feeling of community amongst them. Sue Grafton and other authors picked up those feminist developments and processed social issues in their literature, demonstrating that women can be independent, strong and self-employed. Female detectives such as Sharon McCone, Kinsey Millhone and V.I. Warshawski and alongside real American women broke with the classic stereotype of a woman. But the evolution of the female detective and the feminist movement did not end there.

3.3 Kay Scarpetta: The Modern Female Detective

The early 1990s generally mark the beginning of the third wave of feminism. Although protests and marches may have decreased in frequency, the quest for equality has not eased up. As opposed to the earlier waves of feminism, today's feminist movement deals with "abortion rights, sexual harassment, date rape, […], pay inequities, […]" (Fainsod Katzenstein, 1990, p.2) as well as equal opportunities within the world of employment.

In the last two decades, women have entered male-dominated institutions and professions such as lawyer, police officer, engineer or banker in greater numbers. Representative of the development within the professional world is Patricia Cornwell's female detective Kay Scarpetta. Not only has Scarpetta chosen a male profession but she has attained a leadership position within her field of work– she is the chief medical examiner of Virginia. Even though, "Cornwell wasn't the first woman to write crime novels featuring female protagonists, she was the first to popularize the use of a female medical examiner" (Beahm, 2002, p. 8).

Cornwell's bold choice of career for her main character already suggests that Scarpetta must be a fairly independent self-determined woman. The following section of this paper shall attempt to carefully investigate the Kay Scarpetta series, with special focus on her first novel of the series *Postmortem*.

Similar to Amelia Butterworth, Kay Scarpetta is also pitted against a male counterpart. Pete Marino, who works as a homicide detective, is the responsible police officer in their joint cases. The character of Marino is interesting for various reasons. Firstly, he seems to dislike the protagonist and women in general. In many instances he treats Scarpetta with a chauvinistic attitude and often stares at her "disdainfully" (Cornwell, 2009, p.49). This bigoted attitude may be traced back to the fact that he does not seem to approve of having a female as his superior – a mindset probably shared by more than just a few men. The development of the female detective is an excellent example for the concurrent evolution of the feminist movement and the crime fiction genre. First, in fiction and reality, the title of "detective" was exclusively

15

available for men, just like many other occupations were. Later on, women were admitted more and more into those domains, but still faced discrimination and especially sexism in the workplace - a phenomenon that detectives such as Kinsey Millhone were repeatedly faced with. Lastly, since the end of the second wave of feminism, women were not only permitted to enter, but also succeeded in those formerly male-only employments. Nowadays, regardless of their qualifications and knowledge, leading women like Scarpetta are not always as fully accepted in their work environment as a man in an equal position would be.

Another step that can be traced back to the success of feminism is the new-found self-confidence women gained as feminism evolved. Scarpetta is well aware of the fact that Marino is not too fond of her but does not let that bother her in the least. She remains confident and "offers him a firm and respectful handshake while his eyes went as flat as two tarnished pennies" (Cornwell, 2009, p.27).

In the novel, different men react in different ways when confronted with clear instructions by a woman. Some react with a simple "Yes, ma'am." (Cornwell, 2009, p.22), while others, such as Marino; blatantly disregard her orders (see Cornwell, 2009, p.28). These two responses by fictional characters are reflective of how men in society react when a woman as their superior is in the position to give them orders.

The reason for Scarpetta's confidence cannot only be traced back to the effectiveness of the feminist movement, but is also based on the fact that she is very competent in her profession as a medical examiner. She relies on her set of skills in solving crimes and is fully aware that her intelligence, her experience and her well-developed deductive skills are the reason for her successful career. According to Hans Bertens and Theo D'haen, Scarpetta is "an extraordinarily competent, high-ranking professional who values her independent stance and is easily equal to the males surrounding her" (Bertens/ D'haen, 2001, p. 170). But one can even go one step further and argue that Scarpetta is superior to the men in the novel, especially Marino. During one incident, Marino assumes that the victim's husband is the murderer, while Scarpetta knows

16

that this is unlikely to be true. "Domestic shootings, poisonings, beatings, and stabbings are one thing, but a lust murder is another, not many husbands would have the stomach for binding, raping and strangling their wives" (Cornwell, 2009, p. 28). This shows that the intelligence of women detectives is finally acknowledged, as opposed to being dismissed as sheer luck or intuition, which was the case for earlier female detectives like Amelia Butterworth. Author Susan A. Lichtman states that "women writers tend to break stereotypes and historical presumptions by presenting strong women characters who [...] move from ignorance to knowledge, from inexperience to experience" (Lichtman, 1996, p. 9), which is definitely the case in crime fiction.

The second reason why Marino can be considered interesting for this paper is that he represents the typical hard-boiled detective. He is described as

> *"pushing fifty, with a face life had chewed on, and long wisps of graying hair parted low on one side and combed over his balding pate. At least six feet tall, he was bay-windowed from decades of bourbon or beer. His unfashionably wide red-and-blue-striped tie was oily around the neck from summers of sweat. Marino was the stuff of tough-guy flicks – a crude, crass gumshoe who probably had a foulmouthed parrot for a pet and a coffee table littered with Hustler magazines"* (Cornwell, 2009, p.12-13).

Many of those characteristics can also be found in classical hard-boiled detectives such as Sam Spade and Frank Chambers. Not only is this a clever homage to the roots of crime fiction, but it also highlights the femininity of the protagonist. Patricia Cornwell's Kay Scarpetta "tell[s] us a great deal about how notions of vehement masculinity have become so deeply embedded in the legacy of crime fiction, especially that branch of the genre which lays a claim towards realism" (Bradford, 2015, p 93).

It appears that femininity is now a deliberately used characteristic by authors of crime fiction, rather than being ignored and belittled. Instead of just making room for women in a men's world, a new world is created that "fully reflect[s] the traditional priorities given by women to caring roles, to relationships, to emotional needs and expression" (Ross Nickerson, 2010, p.

158-159). Throughout the novel, many examples can be found which indicate that attributes society usually ascribes to female characters are now desired and emphasized.

Instead of living in a dull gloomy apartment like Kinsey Millhone did, Scarpetta lives in a large home she carefully decorated (see Cornwell, 2009, p33). In addition to interior design she also enjoys gardening and cooking Italian food, hobbies that are usually considered feminine activities as well (see Cornwell, 2009, p.118).

Scarpetta combines domesticity and career well and even shows a motherly side, when she takes care of her niece Lucy over the summer (see Cornwell, 2009, p.6). That these two lifestyles were not always regarded as compatible can be detected in the attitude of Scarpetta's mother who tells her that "[she] should have been a man, […] all work and ambition. It's not natural for a woman" (Cornwell, 2009, p.39). However, her relationship with her niece highlights that family is important to her and shows her caring side, which stands in direct contrast to former female detectives, especially those who imitated hard-boiled detectives, who were detached from traditional family values. The modern woman can now be both, a caring mother figure and a successful businesswoman.

Relationships in general seem to have become more important. In addition to her family, the reader learns that Scarpetta has different love interests throughout the novel. In *Postmortem* she is divorced from her first husband, later she has an insignificant relationship and in *Blowfly* her boyfriend Bento proposes to her. The development of the female detective's love life is of special significance when considering earlier examples of female detectives. From the elderly, almost asexual Miss Butterworth to the hard-boiled female detectives who were either divorced or never married, to a well-rounded female character that has a complex and realistic love life. This development is reflective of the evolvement of actual women's love lives. First, they were not supposed to be considered sexually active individuals or sexual beings at all, but with time women discovered and even celebrated their sexuality - a cause that was fought for during the third wave of feminism.

> *"The introduction of such relationships is not unexpected in a society that has become more open about its discussions of sexuality. It also probably adds to the popularity of the series by introducing an element of romance, thereby, perhaps, widening the appeal of the plot"* (DellaCava/Engel, 1993, p. 18).

Not only have the ways female detectives lead their relationships in general evolved with time, but Scarpetta's love life during the 15 years between the publications of *Postmortem* in 1990 to *Depraved Heart* in 2015 has changed also. At the beginning of the series the reader learns that she was married to Tony Benedetti, whom she met during her studies at university. However, after six years their marriage ended in divorce, because Benedetti had a very traditional image of how a wife is supposed to be. He demanded that Scarpetta quits her profession in order to be a housewife.

In later works of the series, FBI Agent Benton Wesley develops an interest in her. Their relationship is characterized by mutual respect as well as sexual tension. Furthermore, Wesley seems to be appreciative of Scarpetta's (as well as Lucy's) ambition and intelligence, instead of trying to suppress it.

It appears that another parallel can be drawn at this point. The first man of significance in Scarpetta's life bore traditional patriarchal prejudices about what a woman can and cannot do. This mirrors the bogged down image many men had and still have of women. With time this image changed and a woman with a successful career appeared to become not only tolerable, but desirable – a development represented by the character of Benton Wesley.

The fact that literature mirrors the society within it has been created can also be deducted from the newest tendencies in crime fiction. With homosexuality no longer being as much of a taboo, slowly more and more lesbian detectives entered the scene. In fact, the first work of crime fiction with a decidedly homosexual protagonist dates back to as early as 1961, when *Gay Detective* by Lou Rand was published. As the genre matured, the list of gay or lesbian detectives became more substantial. Today over "one hundred series, as well as countless stand-alone mysteries" (Markowitz, 2004, p. 3) can be found.

Pat Welch's protagonist Helen Black from the Helen Black series is one of those lesbian detectives. Welch's novels such as *Murder by the Book* from 1990 are strongly influenced by problems related to homophobia, the cases in the series are often related to homophobic hate crimes (Markowitz, 2004, p. 108). In the second novel of the series *Still Water*, people in Black's environment refer to gays as "queers" and "sick perverts" (DellaCava/ Engel, 1993, p. 34). The father of a lesbian girl even goes as far as letting his daughter die in a fire. As he explains: "If only she'd been like other girls her age. Wanting to get married, have some grandkids [and] spend her life with a good man." (DellaCava/ Engel, 1993, p. 34) However, according to him "she already had the sickness" (DellaCava/ Engel, 1993, p. 34) and deserved to die. He even goes as far as telling Black that if it were up to him, all homosexuals "would have been burned in that fire" (DellaCava/ Engel, 1993, p. 35).

Throughout the series, Black is also confronted with other social issues, like homelessness, police corruption, substance-abuse and racism, just to name a few. As mentioned earlier, society shapes literature. By thematising these sensitive issues, literature raises awareness for social problems and as a direct result also shapes society.

Furthermore, "the broadened context of the novels results from today's female protagonists presenting an image as involved, activist women. They are very much step on with the American woman of the 1990s" (DellaCava/ Engel, 1993, p. 3).

4. Conclusion

The evolution of the female detective has been a remarkable one. The female protagonist started to take shape in the late 18th century out of a completely male-dominated literary character. Amelia Butterworth, a spinster amateur detective, was the first representative for the American female detective, and even inspired Agatha Christie's most well-known character Miss Marple. In the 1980s the female protagonist finally succeeded and gained acknowledgement. The female detectives Kinsey Millhone, as well as Sharon McCone and V.I. Warshawski represent strong, independent women who took on a completely male dominated work field and found their place in it. And lastly, there is Patricia Cornwell's Kay Scarpetta who dominates not only in her area of expertise but also over her male colleagues. In a nutshell, the female detective started out as an amateur, became professional and nowadays can even be found in leading positions. Contemporary writers have shifted from writing about tough detectives and private eyes "and their novels now include interesting women characters who range well beyond the old stereotypes" (Ross Nickerson, 2010, p.161). The progress of feminism has been equally impressive and is closely linked to the evolution of the female detective. From the first wave of feminism, a time of complete political inequality and male dominance, to the 60s and 70s, when women fought for emancipation to today – an era of supposed equality of the genders.

But could gender equality be fully realized, or is it merely a concept that has not been achieved yet? In theory, the feminist movement can be considered successful. It is against the law to discriminate against a person based on their gender. But the genuine truth is that full equality is still a theoretical concept. The numbers do not lie: Although women make up a majority of the US population, namely 58% (see Center of American Progress, 2015), they are less likely to hold a leading position than men (see Center of American Progress, 2015) and even receive a lower salary for the very same work. "In 2014, the typical woman [in the] United States earned only 79 percent of what the typical man earned [...]. Phrased differently, she earned 79 cents for every dollar that he earned" (The White House, 2015).

In the world of literature, a similar phenomenon can be found: In the late 1970s only 166 novels by women writers of mystery fiction were published, while during the early 1990s 1252 works by female authors entered the market (see Walton/Jones, 1999, p. 29). But even though the number of female protagonists and female authors in crime fiction has increased drastically, male authors still win more awards than female authors do. In addition, crime novels featuring a male detective as protagonist also win more awards than those featuring a female protagonist. In the last few years, women have won a significantly lower number of awards than men have. Simply by looking at the most prestigious and therefore most important award in crime fiction, the Edgar Allan Poe Award, one can clearly see that men still overwhelmingly dominate the field. The last three years from 2013 to 2015 male authors as well as male protagonists won the category best novel, it was only this year, in 2016, that a woman author with a female protagonist won the award for best novel (see The Edgars, 2016). But altogether in all categories male authors and protagonists are still in the lead.

The English-American author Nicola Griffith said: "It's about the culture we're embedded in and that's embedded in all of us, women and men. This is the culture that still calls male writers Writers, and female writers Women Writers. The male perspective is still the real one, the standard. Women's voices are just details" (The Guardian, 2015).

However, society is on the right track. For the first time in years, a female author using a female protagonist has won the important Edgar Allan Poe Award for Best Novel. The feminist movement has obviously not reached all of its goals yet; our generation is still fighting for equal treatment and will certainly not stop until full equality is established. The next big step for feminism is already under way: For the first time in history, a woman is running for US president.

5. Bibliography

Primary Literature

Cornwell, Patricia. *The Scarpetta Collection Volume I: Postmortem and Body of Evidence.* New York: Scribner, 2009.

Grafton, Sue. *A is for Alibi.* London: Pan Books, 1993.

Green, Anna Katharine. *The Affair Next Door.* New York: A. L. Burt Company, 1897.

Secondary Literature

Beahm, Georg. *The Unofficial Patricia Cornwell Companion: A Guide to the Bestselling Author's Life and Work.* New York: Minotaur Books, 2002.

Bertens, Hans / D'haen, Theo. *Contemporary American Crime Fiction.* Houndsmill, Basingstoke, Hampshire, New York: PALGRAVE, 2001.

Bradford, Richard. *Crime Fiction: A very short introduction.* Oxford: Oxford University Press, 2015.

Cassuto, Leonard/ Eby, Clare Virginia/ Reiss, Benjamin (ed.) *The Cambridge History of the American Novel.* Cambridge: Cambridge University Press, 2011.

DellaCava, Frances A. / Engel, Madeline H. *Female Detectives in American Novels: A Bibliography and Analysis of Serialized Female Sleuths.* New York, London: Garland Publishing, 1993.

Fainsod Katzenstein, Mary. "Feminism within American Institutions: Unobtrusive Mobilization in the 1980s." *Signs* 16.1 (Autumn, 1990): 27-54.

Gillis, Stacy/ Howie, Gillian/ Munford, Rebecca (ed.) *Third Wave Feminism.* New York: Palgrave, 2007.

Herbert, Rosemary. *The Oxford Companion to Crime and Mystery Writing.* Oxford:Oxford University, 1999.

Humm, Maggie (ed). *Feminisms: A Reader.* New York: Harvester Wheatsheaf, 1992.

Krieg, Alexandra. *Auf Spurensuche: Der Kriminalroman und seine Entwicklungen von den Anfängen bis zur Gegenwart.* Marburg: Tectum Verlag, 2002.

Lerner, Gerda. "Women's Rights and American Feminism." *The American Scholar* 40.2 (Spring 1971): 235-248.

Lichtman, Susan A. *The female hero in women's literature and poetry.* Lewiston, Queenston, Lampeter: The Edwin Mellen Press, 1996.

Maida, Patricia D./ Green, Anna Katharine. "Anna Katharine Green (1846–1935).". *Legacy.* 3.2 (Fall 1986): 53-59.

Markowitz, Judith A. *The Gay Detective Novel: Lesbian and Gay Main Characters and Themes in Mystery Fiction.* Jefferson: McFarland, 2004.

Priestman, Martin. *Detective Fiction and Literature.* Houndsmill, Basingstoke, Hampshire, London: The Macmillan Press, 1990.

Reddy, Maureen T. *Sisters in Crime: Feminism and the Crime Novel.* New York: The Continuum Publishing Company, 1988.

Ross Nickerson, Catherine (ed.) *The Cambridge Companion to American Crime Fiction.* Cambridge: Cambridge University Press, 2010.

Schmidt, Jochen. *Gangster, Opfer, Detektive: Eine Typengeschichte des Kriminalromans.* Frankfurt, M-Berlin: Ulstein GmbH, 1989.

Walton, Priscilla L./ Jones, Manina. *Detective Agency: Women rewriting the hard-boiled tradition.* Berkeley, Los Angeles, London: University of California Press, 1999.

Internet sources

American Rhetoric. 5 Sep. 1995. American Rhetoric. 05.08.2016 <http://www.americanrhetoric.com/speeches/hillaryclintonbeijingspeech.htm>.

Center for American Progress. 4 Aug. 2015. Center for American Progress. 08.08.2016 <https://www.americanprogress.org/issues/women/report/2015/08/04/118743/the-womens-leadership-gap/>.

The Edgars. 28 April 2016. The EDGAR. 08.08.2016 <http://www.theedgars.com/2016EdgarWinners.pdf>.

The Guardian. 01 June 2015. Guardian News and Media Limited. 08.08 2016 <https://www.theguardian.com/books/2015/jun/01/books-about-women-less-likely-to-win-prizes-study-finds>.

The White House. April 2015. The White House. 08.08.2016 <https://www.whitehouse.gov/sites/default/files/docs/equal_pay_issue_brief_final.pdf>.

UN Women. 20 Sep. 2014. UN Women. 05.08.2016 <http://www.unwomen.org/en/news/stories/2014/9/emma-watson-gender-equality-is-your-issue-too>.

Milton Keynes UK
Ingram Content Group UK Ltd.
UKHW011951210823
427215UK00004B/391

9 783346 779717